KT-570-118

Mentoring is a powerful tool in the education and development of sports coaches at all levels. Successful coach development programmes change the behaviour and practice of coaches, whether they are operating at novice or international level. For this change to occur, learning must take place. Much of this resource will focus on how learning occurs and how, as a mentor, you might support coaches' learning. The process of mentoring is difficult to pin down – this is a strength, not a weakness. Mentoring quite simply means a one-to-one relationship supporting the development of another person (coach/volunteer/official). The concept is as broad as necessary and as inclusive as possible.

This resource provides a framework for mentoring. It is not prescriptive, because every mentoring relationship is unique. That is what makes the mentor's task so varied and rewarding. The process outlined is flexible enough to fit comfortably with any mentoring programme designed by governing bodies of sport or other organisations. It should also be utilitarian enough to provide mentors and prospective mentors with guidelines for developing a meaningful relationship, and tools that provide a focus for, and record of, the relationship.

Section One provides a general introduction to mentoring.

Sections Two to Five focus on practical mentoring skills and activities that will increase the effectiveness of your mentoring relationships.

More in-depth knowledge to inform your mentoring practice is provided in Sections Six and Seven.

Section Eight will help you to explore how you might develop your mentor profile and practice.

This resource can stand alone. It also supports a mentoring workshop of the same name[1]. The workshop will help you relate the general ideas and frameworks outlined in this resource to the specific requirements of your sport and your own mentoring relationships. Whether you attend the workshop or not, this resource is your mentor, to help in your learning process as you come to terms with the demands of mentoring. There are many routes into coaching – mentoring can support the induction of the novice as well as fast-track the elite performer into the coaching ranks. Many of the mentoring principles are similar, though the context will be quite different. Whichever area of mentoring you are concerned with, this resource will help explain your role and give you some ideas on how to be most effective as a mentor.

> Mentoring is a practical activity. To get the most from your interaction with the information presented, please take the time to reflect on it and complete the activities that are included. In this way you will be best able to make a judgement on the relevance of the information to you and your own mentoring practice.

Contents

> *I can't describe how good I felt at that moment I had learned and he had learned, but there was no one there to take credit. There was only the glimmer of a realisation that we were both participating in a wonderful process.*
>
> Gallwey, 1986

What is Mentoring?

Think of someone who has had a strong positive influence on your coaching. Perhaps it was someone you admired and worked with; maybe it was someone with whom you could discuss your coaching problems. Whether or not you realised it at the time, you had a mentor. In many cases, mentors are not recognised for what they are – often a mentoring experience will only be obvious when you look back on it from a distance.

Other mentors will be more obvious as you will have chosen them, or they will have been assigned to you for a specific purpose.

The following activity will help you identify someone who has filled the mentor role for you and the impact she has had on your development.

Mentor is derived from a Greek word meaning trusted adviser or friend.

Think about...

- someone who has had a strong positive influence on your development:

- what influence they had on you:

Most people have been mentored by somebody at some stage in their life. The mentoring role can range from someone showing you the ropes in a new job to a close friend you may turn to for advice.

There is no set pattern for a mentoring relationship. Each one is unique to the individuals involved.

What Does a Mentor Do?

Mentors can be assigned or may develop informally from friendships and working relationships. A mentoring relationship may accomplish many things, or focus on just one area of development – mentoring experiences may last for a week or a lifetime.

In this resource, you will see that although different types of relationships will have different nuances and emphases, mentoring experiences are essentially the same. Mentoring is a process rather than an event. Mentors must see themselves as facilitators of a process, rather than as teachers or educators of the coach.

Mentors can adopt many different roles and styles. These will be considered in more detail in the later sections. An example of some roles are listed below:

Mentors can:

- be a role model (someone whose styles/methods are copied)

- build confidence (encourage the coach to believe in himself)

- be a resource (provide information and give direction to where help can be found)

- develop knowledge or skills (act as a coach)

- challenge and question (confront beliefs and values).

One of your biggest challenges as a mentor is to ensure your mentoring remains relevant to the coach. This means allowing the coach to set the agenda and pace for the relationship. The beliefs and values you have developed to guide your own coaching are important frames of reference for you. Other coaches will benefit from exposure to them, as you benefit from discovering their beliefs and values. However, you must ensure you do not impose them on your relationship with another coach.

Allowing your beliefs and values to surface raises the possibility of a disagreement, and this can be a distraction from the main business of mentoring. When you say something contrary to the opinion of the coach you are mentoring, they may begin to question the relevance of your input to their needs or even your commitment to keeping those needs, rather than your own, at the top of the agenda. Of course at a later stage in the relationship, when you know the coach well, debate can be a useful medium for exploring a coach's point of view.

When you have strong beliefs and values it is difficult to be non-evaluative in your responses to another coach's statements and opinions. Remember your task as mentor is not to preach, inform or teach, but to assist a coach to clarify their own personal set of values and beliefs. If they do not mirror yours, all the better – you are both richer for the shared experience.

Range of Mentoring Experiences

It should be obvious by now that mentoring covers many different types of experiences and relationships. These can be described on a continuum between highly structured mentoring programmes (perhaps part of a formal qualifications programme) and informal relationships or friendships (Figure 1).

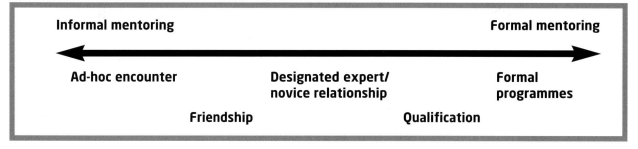

Figure 1: The mentoring process

Mentoring and Coach Education Programmes

Coach education experiences often occur in isolated blocks of time, usually several months or even years apart. For some coaches, coach education is a means rather than an end – it is a progression up the coaching ladder by obtaining a qualification.

In general, coach education programmes remove coaches from their surroundings and transport them to a centralised location. There, they will be fed information and applications that are relevant and important to their coaching. Yet in an Australian study (Douge et al., 1994), it was shown that while coaches do increase their knowledge, they rarely improve their coaching effectiveness after attendance at a coach education course. The findings of Douge et al. highlight a gap in form and context between a coach education course and the actual practice of coaching.

Coach education programmes operate under constraints of time and resources. Introductory and foundation courses are often attended by a widely dispersed audience as most participants are volunteer coaches, therefore they are limited in the amount of time and money they can devote to furthering their coaching expertise. Many governing bodies of sport and other coach educators attempt to bridge these gaps in various ways, including:

- making coach education courses as practical as possible in content and activities

- involving coaches in coaching (peer coaching or with invited performers) on coach education courses

- ensuring a number of hours of practical coaching are logged in the post-course period

- decentralising courses and making them modular (in manageable segments) instead of overloading coaches with information over one weekend

- incorporating a period of supervised experience as part of their coach education programmes

- organising a mentoring programme parallel to the coach education programme

- encouraging coaches to work in pairs as they gain experience.

The Coach Education Gap

Form: Much of the material that coach educators wish to transmit is theoretical; however, coaching is a practical activity. This means there is a large leap for coaches to make between the material received and their own practice.

Context: Coach education courses occur in a centralised location, usually separate from the coach's delivery environment and performers. This leap of context can be very difficult for the coach to make. Things that seemed to make complete sense at the coach education course suddenly become more complex and difficult when coaches attempt to implement them with their performers or team.

Learning Experiences

Coaches learn in many different ways. Consider how you improved as a coach. Very often, learning experiences are accidents – a chance discussion with another coach, a visit to see a senior coach's session, or an observation at a competition. These experiences do not lend themselves to planned programmes of development. The challenge for a mentor is to encourage the coach to use these experiences to build on the formal coach education programme.

Such learning experiences can be very exciting for a coach. Think of how you feel, even now, when you know you have grasped the solution – do you get a sense of achievement? Do you feel you can contribute in new and better ways to the development of your performers?

Mentoring is about such moments. It is the tremendously satisfying job of helping coaches to improve their coaching – it is about creating and magnifying learning experiences.

Mentoring does not revolve around advising or providing solutions. Mentoring means different things to different people at different levels. With novice coaches, mentoring may be about empowering and helping coaches to control the learning process for themselves. With experienced coaches, it may focus on challenging the beliefs and values they have developed so they come to a deeper understanding of their roles and tasks. In every case, the learning process is a keystone of the mentoring relationship.

Think about...

- an experience that improved your coaching:

  - What made this a **learning** experience?

  - Did you find a solution to a problem that had been troubling you for some time?

  - Was some information communicated to you in a particularly effective way?

  - Were you inspired by somebody you especially respect in a certain area of expertise?

Mentors help coaches recognise and maximise learning opportunities.

Learning comes in many different guises. Sometimes, coaches cannot recognise the learning opportunities that lurk within the problems, chance occurrences and run-of-the-mill events that happen almost every day. If coaches do learn from these experiences, it is often by accident. For many coaches, learning is a formal event confined to once or twice a year at a coach education course. Mentors can help coaches recognise and grasp the learning opportunities that happen every day. Your task as a mentor is to help make coaches' learning experiences less accidental.

Finding and Using Information

The way a coach obtains and utilises new information is vital to their learning journey.

In order to develop, coaches must first of all discover new skills and knowledge but, secondly, and most crucially, they must incorporate new skills and knowledge into their practice in an effective way. Finding the information is often the easy part.

- Coaches are informed about new skills and presented with new information at coach education courses.

- Coaches often pick up information from watching and listening to other coaches or sports scientists (both from their own sport and other sports), and from reading resources and journals.

- Analysis of their own and others' performances is an important source of information for coaches.

- Trial and error is one of the most common ways for a coach to discover new methods. Through experimentation they will have decided on what works and what does not.

Think about...

- the sources of information that have helped you learn as a coach.

As a coach mentor, **you** may be a source of knowledge for other coaches. If coaches do not know something they need to know, they may ask you for help or you may volunteer the information. You may refer them to another source of information such as a book, video, course or another coach. In this way, you can impart some of the benefits of your knowledge and experience in a certain area. This is only the initial stage of the mentoring process, however. As a mentor, your major task is to facilitate the process by which coaches use such information to **change their current coaching practice**.

How Do You Know When Coaches Have Learnt?

When you coach performers, you look for a **permanent change in their behaviour** to indicate they have learnt a new skill. Think about all the time you spend as a coach measuring and monitoring your performer(s) to identify whether the changes you aim to effect in performance have occurred.

While it is relatively easy to measure and evaluate sports performance, coaching performance is not so easy to gauge. There is no time, score or other objective scale to indicate whether coaching is good or bad. Many coaches measure their own effectiveness by improvements in their performers. This may tell a coach if he is effective (though even then, the connection is tenuous) but does not indicate any improvement over past coaching performance.

Changing Current Practice

Coaching is a practical activity and in many ways it is similar to performing. Just because you read a resource on swimming it does not necessarily mean you will be able to swim in a technically correct manner – that will require you to apply the information from the resource to your current abilities. The knowledge without application will not be enough. Similarly with coaching, knowledge alone is not sufficient. Coaches must apply that knowledge to their coaching behaviour in order to become more effective coaches.

Coach Education as a Source of Knowledge

In the past, coach education courses worked on the principle that learning theoretical knowledge will lead to a change in behaviour (Figure 2).

Figure 2: The link between theory and practice

The Theory-practice Link

Newly acquired knowledge must be **applied** to coaching practice in order to change it. For example, in teacher training, most training courses will require students to undergo a period of time in teaching practice – an opportunity to apply the principles and theory they have studied to a period of supervised performance in the teacher role. Coaches learn in a similar way.

It is in the time immediately following the course or discovery of new information that any change to the learner's practice is likely to occur. During this period, coaches need encouragement and assistance to apply the theoretical information they have gained to their practice. This is the time in which the advice and encouragement of a mentor can be most effective.

More Than Just Passing on Knowledge

The mentor-coach relationship does not have to involve a very experienced coach and an inexperienced one, neither is it ever just one-way traffic. Indeed, the benefits to the coaching practice of the mentor are often as great as the benefits to the coach.

Very often, a mentor will meet a coach for the first time following a coach education course. The coach is probably full to the brim with new pieces of information and ideas. The mentor, rather than add to this load, must help the coach with the application of the knowledge and theories to the practice of coaching.

Mentoring relationships can and do develop between coaches of equal standing. Through discussion and reflection, insights can be shared and evaluated. The different strengths of coaches at a similar level often complement each other. The technical knowledge of a coach who has competed at a high level can be complemented by a coach who has a background in teaching or sports science, for example. Sharing ideas with other coaches at the same level can help coaches solve problems and broaden their perspectives. Indeed, it can sometimes be easier for coaches at a similar level to communicate with each other openly. It is also important to note that coaches can learn from 'less experienced' coaches, who may possess a diverse range of skills, knowledge, experience and qualities that may impact on their own coaching.

Summary

Mentoring is about strengthening the link between knowing and doing. Coaching is a practical activity, and mentoring is an important tool to help coaches improve their practice. The following sections will help you work with coaches to assess their needs and help them take responsibility for their own learning.

Think about...

- your coach education experiences; how much of your learning as a coach is directly attributable to formal courses?

- what proportion of your development as a coach is from practical experiences such as watching others and problem solving, and to what extent you have learnt by applying theory from resources and courses to your practice.

The rose is a rose from the time it is a seed to the time it dies. Within it, at all times it contains its whole potential. It seems to be constantly in the process of change; yet at each stage, at each moment, it is perfectly all right as it is.

Gallwey, 1986

The Mentor's Supporting Role

As a coach, when working with athletes, do you tend to take a leading role? Do you know what is right for them, so you advise them strongly and even make decisions for them? Coaches have a tendency to think they know best. Of course, this is often true. Athletes look to coaches for guidance, and can feel more focused when decisions are made for them in a training or competition environment.

A coach:player relationship is very different to a mentor:coach relationship. Your job is not to **advise** the coach or to **fix** her coaching (see 'Giving Feedback' in Section Four, page 21). It is important you enter a mentoring situation with a very open mind – leave behind the mindset you have developed for your own coaching. This mindset may have guided you well through your development as a coach, but it may not be appropriate for another coach. Be careful not to subconsciously impose your own values and beliefs on your relationship with another coach.

Beware of statements such as:

- 'I have always found in that situation...'

- 'What works best for me is...'

- 'What you should do...'

These may be indications that the relationship is being driven by your perspective and not that of the coach.

The most common cause of failure in a mentoring relationship is lack of **empathy**. You will find it very easy to advise a coach on what to do to improve the areas of performance that are weakest – in your opinion. Your opinion is formed by your experience and your priorities – it is not necessarily the only, or best, opinion.

Every coach has a subjective perspective on their priorities and abilities. Unless you can understand this perspective, you will be unable to contribute meaningfully to the coach's self-analysis and you run the risk of providing irrelevant advice.

> *Empathy – the power of identifying with (and so fully comprehending) a person.*

Motives to Mentor

Being part of a successful mentoring relationship can provide as many fruitful experiences for the mentor as it can the coach. To maximise development from these opportunities it is important a mentor understands their motives behind taking on a mentoring commitment.

There are numerous reasons why people choose to become mentors. These include:

- a desire to 'give something back'

- to be part of an organisational culture

- for the satisfaction of passing on knowledge

- to acquire new knowledge/learn more about themselves

- to expand a personal network.

Understanding your motives for mentoring will, in turn, inform your 'mentoring philosophy' and build a solid foundation upon which to base a new mentor:coach relationship.

Stages of a Mentoring Relationship

The mentoring journey can be divided into four clear stages and you may progress through the stages at different speeds – some may even advance through two stages at the same time.

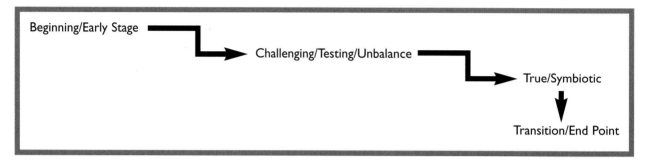

Figure 3: The stages of a mentoring relationship

Beginning/Early Stage

Mentoring relationships must be developed. As with any relationship, the initial stage is very much a sounding-out stage, with both participants assessing the other. It may be at this stage that the coach has an ideal picture of you, the mentor, and the mentoring relationship. The coach may have expectations of the relationship that are not concurrent with your approach. You must make your role as facilitator very clear in the initial stage, and encourage the coach to take responsibility for their own learning from the start.

It can be useful at an early stage to explore the expectations of both the mentor and the coach. This can pre-empt problems that may occur at a later stage due to incompatible expectations. It places the relationship on a strong footing, and will indicate some areas of priority that need to be addressed.

> **Mentor Priorities**
>
> Clarifying coach expectations
>
> Agreeing priorities
>
> Developing empathy
>
> Observation

Challenging/Testing/Unbalance

Some mentoring relationships are convened for a specific purpose – to prepare for an assessment or work through a specific task or programme. Others are open-ended relationships. Often, such relationships will follow a familiar cycle of decreasing involvement, as the coach becomes more familiar with the material and more confident in making decisions – therefore less inclined to ask for advice.

In the initial stages, the relationship is likely to be an unbalanced one. You may have knowledge and experience that the learner coach does not. You may often feel the need to explain, give information and sometimes advice. You may find yourself filling the role of counsellor and resource provider.

> **Mentor Priorities**
>
> Share knowledge
>
> Guide coach to solutions
>
> Encourage reflection
>
> Reassure

True/Symbiotic

As the coach develops in knowledge and confidence, the relationship may develop into a two-way process of personal development. The coach learns how to manage the self-reflection process and becomes adept at learning from experience. Contacts become less formal and perhaps less frequent, although the relationship can still be strong. Your role changes to one that assists, rather than directs, the learning process. Coaches and mentors may attend competitions together as learning experiences, or they may discuss issues that concern them as equal partners. These relationships can progress into strong friendships.

> **Mentor Priorities**
>
> Development planning
>
> Reflection
>
> Monitoring progress
>
> Giving feedback

Transition/End Point

The mentor:coach relationship will usually have a natural end point, whether it is the completion of a formal programme or that the mentor feels they have added enough value to the coach's practice and thinking. Many mentors remain familiar with coaches they have worked with, usually as friends or informal advisers.

Assessor/Mentor Conflict

The roles of assessor and mentor can be difficult to reconcile. As a mentor you will seek to generate empathy with the learner coach. This requires openness and honesty on behalf of both mentor and coach. This openness and honesty can be quite difficult to achieve when the coach is aware of your role as assessor. Coaches may find it hard to openly discuss areas in which they believe their performance to be below par.

The roles are not irreconcilable, although if asked (eg by a governing body of sport) to fill both roles, you will need to weigh the relative importance of each very carefully. Their relative weight will, to a large extent, be reflected in the type of relationship you will develop with the coach.

Building Rapport

Effective mentoring requires an open, trusting and honest relationship between mentor and mentee. Only when this relationship is formed can you develop a real empathy with your mentee and help unlock their potential. Building rapport and developing a good working relationship are at the heart of the mentoring process. Hildebrand (2007) identified four areas that contribute towards rapport developing between a mentee and mentor.

1 Commonalities Shared ideas, traits and interests will develop a relationship on a common, shared foundation. Finding these commonalities will involve sharing and communication.	**2 Connectivity** Once sharing has taken place and commonalities have been discovered, a connection will be made.
3 Communication Developing rapport through communication is not simply the words you use. It involves body language, gestures and eye contact.	**4 Collaboration** You must develop shared approaches to the structure, outcomes and approach to your relationship.

Figure 4: The 4Cs for building rapport

Barriers to Mentoring

Whether real or perceived, several barriers may exist to successful mentoring. These may include:

- trust of the mentor

- suspicion

- fear of criticism

- complacency

- fear of rejection

- ownership of the process.

This is not intended to be an exhaustive list. There may be other key areas that could become barriers to the mentoring process. Recognising such obstacles will help to ensure they are avoided.

Summary

Building good relationships and developing rapport are central to effective mentoring. In developing a positive working relationship, acquiring a better understanding of your coach is not always an easy task, but it is important to find out more about them and let them know they can discuss their worries or concerns with you. Value their contributions – they have much to offer. Doing this will make your role as a mentor easier and it can help build confidence and a feeling of worth for the relationship.

© sports coach UK

*By the word **learning**, I do not mean the collection of information but the realisation of something which actually changes your behaviour.*

Gallwey, 1986

Be Relevant

Mentoring involves interacting with coaches to improve their coaching. When you are working with coaches you will sometimes be involved in coaching activities or conversations that relate directly to a particular coaching problem.

Your input must be relevant to the immediate learning needs (and wants) of the coach, otherwise you will both have a frustrating experience. The assessment of these needs requires you to have a knowledge of learning theory, but also an honest dialogue with the coach, and maintain an open relationship where you both feel free to make comments and suggestions. As a mentor, you need to address both of these areas.

Stages of Coach Growth

The development needs of every coach will be different. Every mentoring relationship is a unique challenge for the mentor. However, the role you adopt will be determined to some extent by the stage of development of the coach you are mentoring. There are various stages of learning a new role – coaches at the different stages will have different needs and you will need different skills and qualities to meet these needs.

Novice coaches will, in the initial stages, **model** coaching behaviour – they will try to recreate the behaviour of another coach they admire or look up to. This modelling will be based on their own experience of being coached or of observing other coaches, or perhaps on the basis of instructions given at a coach education course.

© Alan Edwards

When coaches become aware of a set of skills and behaviours that underpin the behaviour they are modelling, they will attempt to progress to the stage of **competency** in them. These skills and behaviours are not the coach's own discovery – they will usually have been prescribed by one, or a combination, of the models the coach has adopted in the early stage.

© Alan Edwards

When they reach the stage of competency in this behaviour, coaches may begin to **reflect on or question** their coaching behaviour more deeply. This reflective process should eventually lead to the formation of an individual's own coaching model. The model will consist of a set of beliefs and values that have been developed through coaching experiences. As this personal model develops, coaches tend to move towards a stage of **autonomy**, where they judge all new inputs and experiences against a strongly formed set of beliefs and values.

These stages are summarised in Table 1.

Table 1: Learning stages

Stage of Learning	Learner Characteristics
Modelling	Needs a prescribed set of routines and skills. The coach will attempt to copy behaviours.
Competency	The coach aims for mastery of a set of skills.
Reflection	The creation of a personal model for coaching based on a set of values and beliefs. This involves reflection on the learner's own, and investigation of others', coaching practice.
Autonomy	The reflection and enquiry of the earlier stage have resulted in a strongly held set of beliefs and values that create a context for the assimilation of all new information and activities.

These different stages can correspond very loosely to coaching levels. Be careful though, as a novice coach with lots of experience as a captain or senior performer may transfer a significant amount of knowledge and skill from performing to coaching. This individual might already be at the reflective stage of coaching. However, many coaches will start at the modelling stage, assuming the methodology and practice of coaches they have worked with or under.

It is also possible for a coach who has achieved **autonomy** to revert back to the **modelling** or **competency** stage if they are faced with a new learning group, skill or environment that they have not operated in or with previously.

Think about...

- identifying four different coaches you know, one for each of the learning stages, and write down a few of the ways they display the characteristics of each stage:

Name:

Modelling:

Name:

Competency:

Name:

Reflection:

Name:

Autonomy:

The Mentor Role Throughout Learning

You should be aware of the needs of the coaches you are mentoring so you can adapt your behaviour and be most effective in your role. Possible mentor roles for the different stages are outlined in Table 2.

Table 2: Mentor roles at different learning stages

Stage of Learning	Mentor Role	Mentor Skills
Modelling	Providing a model Being observed Co-coaching	Demonstrating competence Explaining/teaching
Competency	Coach	Observing Giving feedback Facilitating reflection
Reflection	Facilitator Challenger	Objective support Questioner Managing learning
Autonomy	Partner/co-enquirer	Communicating

Your task is to make each experience a developmental one. Whatever the learning stage of the coach, you must relate the experience to his needs. Your task is to help coaches discover how new experiences and knowledge relate to their current practice as coaches, so they will change their coaching behaviour for the better. This may mean improving or refining skills (particularly at the competency stage), challenging the basis for their current practice (usually at the reflection stage) or experimenting with new methods (autonomy stage).

Mentoring Activities

As a mentor in an official mentoring programme, you will usually be expected to attend coaching sessions taken by the coach you are mentoring. This gives you an opportunity to observe the coach in action, which can help you to understand her strengths and weaknesses. Be careful not to assume the role of the assessor during these visits. You may have criteria set by the programme coordinator, but ensure your observing of the coach is done in a way that they do not feel any pressure to perform differently to their norm. Although many coach qualification programmes may require a mentor to observe a coach presenting a session, coaching sessions are not the only opportunities for mentoring.

The structure you use to guide the mentoring session can help to ensure the learning potential of the experience is fully utilised.

A mentoring session can take place around many other types of activities, such as:

- attending a competition/ event together

- video analysis of a coaching session

- video analysis of a performer/team

- planning programmes or sessions

- observing another coach/sport together.

If you do not know the coach well, a phone call can be difficult as it limits the type and quality of communication (see 'Active Listening' on page 22). As the relationship develops, however, telephone conversations may be a more acceptable form of communication. They are convenient and not very time-consuming.

These and other experiences can provide useful opportunities for mentoring. When coach and mentor are better acquainted, telephone calls, emails and other informal communication can be useful forms of interaction.

Some of these experiences may be more suited to one stage of learning than another. The stage of development of the coach you are mentoring may dictate the type of activity you both prefer. For example, in the competency stage, it may be useful for you to observe the coach in action as often as possible and give objective feedback (just as you do with performers).

Mentoring Interventions

A mentoring intervention generally has the following general structure:

- pre-session meeting

- observation/activity

- post-session analysis and evaluation

- action points.

This structure is a useful guide in the early stages of a relationship. As the relationship develops, it may not be necessary to use this formal process for **every** mentoring meeting and you may be able to split the process into a number of meetings/phone calls.

The Initial Meeting

The first meeting of a mentoring relationship is an important one. The first pre-session meeting must be an ice-breaker, if coach and mentor are not well acquainted.

Practical topics for discussion to set the scene for future meetings should:

- include time constraints on mentor and coach

- set boundaries and air any concerns

- raise confidentiality/conflict issues.

There may be a need to put in place a mentoring agreement. An example of one is given overleaf.

© sports coach UK

Be Prepared

The initial mentoring session can be difficult for both mentor and coach. Coaches usually feel their performance is under review, so it can be an ego-threatening situation. Mentors may feel under pressure to be founts of wisdom and may worry that their performance will not measure up to the expectations of the coach. Following the steps outlined here can help minimise the potential for disharmony.

A Simple Mentoring Agreement

The undersigned do hereby agree to enter into a mentoring relationship for a period of XX years.

_____

The mentee's goals for this relationship are:

• _____

The parties hereby agree and acknowledge:

• to be available for consultation by telephone or email during regular business hours, and occasionally in person

• to meet in person quarterly to review the progress of the relationship and to discuss how the relationship can be improved

• that they will meet in person to deal with any events or circumstances that make continuing the relationship difficult or awkward

• that all matters discussed in the course of the relationship shall be confidential, unless both parties agree that disclosure can occur.

_____ as mentor.

Date: _____

_____ as mentee.

Date: _____

Initial meetings tend to be more formal than informal, as the coach and mentor may not know each other very well. In many senses, they will frame the relationship so an awareness of some key issues can help you make the first meeting a positive one.

There are three important initial tasks that must be undertaken early in the relationship. You may wish to tackle these in the very first meeting, or over two or three sessions, depending on the time you have. By ensuring they are tackled early in the relationship, you can help to create a positive atmosphere. The tasks are:

• clarifying expectations

• agreeing priorities

• establishing a goal.

© SWpix.com

Clarifying Expectations

It is vitally important to clarify the expectations the coach has of the mentor. If the expectations of the coach conflict with the role you envisage for yourself, the stage is set for a very unsatisfactory relationship from both perspectives. Don't dodge this issue, ask the coach: 'What would you like me to be able to do for you?' The ensuing conversation is likely to clear up any misconceptions, while ensuring the relationship is formed around the needs of the coach.

Your task as a mentor is to empower coaches. If they do not understand your aims in this process, they may expect you to fill the role of the conventional teacher. If you have explained your perceptions of your role fully to them in advance, this will be avoided.

> Roles develop through interaction. You should not have too fixed an idea of either your role or the coach's role in the process. With some coaches you will need to take a leading role in the relationship, but as the coach grows in confidence and ability, you should allow him to take the lead. With others you will adopt a supporting role from the start.

Agreeing Priorities

At the outset, you should discuss the coach's development priorities (the areas they see as most important). You may have a conflicting opinion on the coach's strengths and weaknesses but your agenda is not the important one and should not be allowed to dominate. If your input is to be meaningful and relevant to the coach, it must refer to those areas that they have identified as important.

> The importance of this part of the session cannot be overemphasised. Unless you have agreed on priorities, any advice or criticism you offer can be deemed worthless or interfering, as it may not be directed towards an area prioritised by the coach. Such feelings will undermine the entire relationship.

Establishing a Goal

Based on these priorities, set a goal to provide a focus for the session. This will be based on a particular weakness of the coach. Setting this goal at the outset will prevent discussions becoming vague and generalised. It will provide a benchmark against which the effectiveness of the session can be assessed.

Once the formalities have been agreed, the mentor should guide the conversation towards what the coach wants and needs from the relationship.

Using a coach-led approach, the areas to be addressed in this session could include:

- current level of coaching and any qualifications gained

- profile of performer/team

- coaching aims/coaching philosophy

- current coaching strengths and weaknesses – self-assessment

- areas prioritised for development/ self-improvement goals

- coaching ambitions

- attitude towards observer – nervousness can often be transmitted as belligerence, overconfidence or shyness; your assessment of their reaction to you might direct you towards a more informal approach.

The Mentoring Experience

Your role in the mentoring experience will vary, depending on the experience itself and the coach. Perhaps you will merely observe the coach in action, or maybe you will observe another coach or a competition. The coach may even be observing you. Whatever the situation, you should adopt a supporting role, allowing the coach to manage and direct the experience for himself. You may need to demonstrate strong observation or communication skills (see Section Four for details of these skills).

The important period for learning will follow the activity or experience. It is then that your mentoring skills will be required to encourage the coach to **reflect** on the experience and plan to improve future behaviour on the basis of this reflection.

Summary

A mentoring session must be well structured if it is to be successful in maximising learning. It is important you use the initial stages to assess the learner's needs. For your input to be relevant and useful to the coach, it must be informed by a knowledge of the coach's stage of learning and the priorities she identifies for development. This can then allow you to promote and inform a process of self-reflection that is central to learning from experience.

> **Think about...**
>
> - the steps you can take to make mentoring situations as informal/natural as possible.

Clearly, positive and negative evaluations are relative to each other. It is impossible to judge one event as positive without seeing other events as not positive, or as negative...ending judgement means that you neither add nor subtract from the facts before your eyes...

Gallwey, 1986

Essential Skills

This section will look more closely at some of the essential skills you will need to fulfil the role of mentor as outlined in the previous section. The essential skills of mentoring are:

- observation
- giving feedback
- active listening
- questioning.

Good coaches often have good observation skills and an ability to communicate well. You may already demonstrate proficient skills in these areas. However, the observation and communication skills you use as a coach might be different from those required of a mentor. This section will help you examine your skills in these areas and apply them to a mentoring situation.

Observation

Observation is a necessary part of the mentoring relationship. You will remember from Section One that effective learning is about changes in behaviour – it is very difficult to demonstrate this in conversation.

Skilled observation of the coach in action can make your input more focused and effective. First-hand experience will provide you with a clearer perspective on the coach's strengths, weaknesses and approach to coaching than any amount of interviews and discussions.

> Observation may be a particularly relevant skill for a mentor when coaches are at the modelling or competency stage of learning (see page 14).

© Mark Bullimore

Skilled observation has a number of requirements:

- Knowledge of the coach's aims for the session – it is useful to discuss the action to be observed with the coach beforehand. This will enable the mentor to have a context for observation.

- An indication of the type and standard of competences required at the level of the coach you are observing – if the coach is completing a governing body of sport award or other qualification, the competences required for that level will be available and **you should know and understand them**. Very often these competences will be the focus of attention for the coach; therefore, feedback should, where possible, be centred around developing the coach.

- The ability to minimise the strain of being observed, so coaches will not feel under pressure – if they do, they may adapt their behaviour from their norm to what they believe is preferred by the mentor. People differ in achievement motivation and will react differently to an observation situation. Some may see the process as a threat to their ego, others will see it as an opportunity to impress. Both types may alter their usual patterns of behaviour. Adopting a minor role in the activity can help break down barriers. Otherwise, distance is the best method of lessening intrusion.

- Some method of recording thoughts/making notes on the actions of the learner, such as a clipboard or Dictaphone, can be useful in providing a context for the following discussion. Some learners could be intimidated by the presence of a clipboard – it may seem like an assessment situation. A Dictaphone or an unobtrusive card or notebook for recording thoughts may be less threatening.

- Very often you will be expected to complete a form specified by your governing body of sport or programme manager, grading or commenting on competences of the coach. This is often best filled out in consultation with the coach, after he has the opportunity to explain and justify his actions. Areas of disagreement could be left blank for later reflection, or judgement postponed for a later visit. If you visit merely to complete the form, you are an assessor rather than a mentor.

Use Video

If you can arrange to video a coaching session, you will be able to observe the session with the coach. This can provide the coach with a new perspective on herself that can be illuminating – and far more convincing than feedback from a mentor. Observing a session together allows the coach the opportunity to outline the rationale for their interventions as you watch.

Giving Feedback

Feedback is the process of receiving information on actions and it is an important part of learning. More experienced coaches are adept at extracting their own feedback – they have already reached the stage of reflection (see Section Two). Less experienced coaches often find it difficult to evaluate their progress objectively, or to identify areas of difficulty. They must be guided towards the relevant pieces of information.

As coaches become adept at using the self-reflection process, they will find it easier to be objective about their coaching. In the initial stages, you will need to help coaches through the first stage of the reflective cycle (description) towards an objective viewpoint.

Often, a coach will ask for feedback on the coaching session. Giving feedback is a critical skill for the mentor. It is important, however, that the session is not seen by either party as a monologue – remember the process of self-reflection. Feedback may be given in a number of ways:

- **Criticism** is evaluative by nature and it can be difficult to take, whether or not it is constructive. Think of how you react to criticism, even if it is well meaning. This is because criticism focuses on a problem rather than a solution. Criticism is only ever useful if it is focused on an aspect of coaching that is a priority for development in the eyes of the coach. The initial session to set the agenda is key to being able to offer any constructive criticism. If you criticise in an area that is not a priority for development, your entire input is devalued. Whatever the case, use criticism sparingly.

- **Praise** can be useful to improve a coach's confidence. Remember though that praise is the flip side of criticism. By identifying an action as good, you will automatically assign a tag of bad to the opposite. These labels can be counterproductive, because once you begin to judge actions by these criteria, it becomes difficult to focus on effectiveness. Try to use effectiveness or consequence as the basis for evaluation, rather than the tags of good or bad.

- **Advice** is directive and assumes a right way of doing things. Remember that your task is not to generate a clone of your coaching philosophy but to help coaches develop in the way most appropriate to them and their principles of coaching.

- **Guided self-discovery** is less directive and evaluative than the other options. It requires the mentor to use listening and questioning skills carefully. The mentor allows the learner to lead the session. Open questions (see later in this section) are used so that the feedback is non-directive.

Objective feedback is important in the process of reflection. Coaches can find it difficult to view their experiences objectively if they are new to reflection. Objectivity is a skill that develops with time. A coach can obtain feedback from a variety of sources. Trusted performers can be useful sources of feedback that can help coaches to move outside their own limited perceptions of their actions. Helping coaches to be objective in their self-reflection can also be a key role for the mentor.

> Feedback can be a very important skill for a mentor when dealing with coaches at the competence and/or reflective stages of learning (see page 14).

Active Listening

Listening is one of the key skills required by a mentor. Very often when you listen to other people speak, you will find you are both listening to what they are saying and phrasing your response to it. The speaker does not receive your full attention and because of this, you do not receive the full context and content of the message. You can think much faster than the speaker can talk, but in doing this you run the risk of missing important points.

Active listening is central to the communication process. As you receive a spoken message, you interpret it. This requires you to listen to the speaker's words and understand them, as well as paying attention to tone of voice, body language and facial expressions. Often these can hold more meaning than the words the speaker uses. They can explain the context in which the words are used and add meaning to the message beyond the scope of the words.

> **Tips for Active Listening**
>
> Taking occasional notes is an effective means of maintaining concentration on the speaker's message without having to concentrate on your proposed response.
>
> Don't be afraid to pause for thought before you speak – this is not off-putting for the listener.

The process of communication is outlined in Table 3.

Table 3: The process of communication

Stage	Process	Potential Problems
Message	Speaker decides what he wants to communicate	Lack of confidence may result in inaccurate communication
Encode*	Speaker translates this into words and/or signals in the mind	Limitations of vocabulary; cultural/regional differences
Speech	Includes body and sign language as well as tone and pitch of voice	Inhibitions; range of communication skills
Listen	Includes picking up nuances of tone/pitch and body language	Hearing errors; regional/dialect differences
Interpret*	You infer the meaning you think the speaker intended	Ambiguity/assumptions; incorrect inferences
Evaluate	You decide how you wish to respond based on your agenda	If your agenda is different to that of the mentee
Plan response	Encode	Mentee's expectation of time taken to respond may leave them disappointed
Respond	Verbalise response	Response can be misinterpreted depending on vocabulary and body language used

* The most important stages are encoding and interpreting. Think how often you cannot find the words to express precisely what you mean. Even when you believe you do, a seemingly straightforward message is open to misinterpretation. Think of the many alternative meanings and shades of meaning words have in different contexts, areas and professions.

Action Point

The good listener will guard against misinterpretation by paraphrasing the speaker's message as it was received, at intervals, in the conversation and after important statements. This involves repeating the speaker's message back to her. It ensures there is no misunderstanding and can help the speaker to clarify her thoughts. It will very often prompt an elaboration of the message from the speaker.

Body Language

Be aware of your body language. Mehrabian (1968) argued that when your words and body language or paralanguage (eg tone, volume, pitch) are incongruent, words only constitute 7% of the message conveyed. Remember, **LESS** is more:

Lean towards the speaker

maintain **E**ye contact

Smile

Stay relaxed.

Focus on positive signs – eye contact, posture (lean towards the speaker) and expression (smiles, nods and so on).

Applications for Mentors

Words – ensure that the words you use are positive and show that you are interested in the mentee. Try to avoid challenging words such as 'why' or giving your opinion on sensitive matters.

Tone – be aware of the tone of your voice. Ensure it portrays you as interested and positive throughout.

Facial expressions – ensure you maintain good eye contact with the mentee throughout the session. Be conscious of what message your face is portraying as it may conflict with what you are actually feeling.

Avoid obvious signs of disinterest like yawning and gazing around the room.

Atmosphere

Create the right atmosphere. Make it obvious this is an important time for you, not time stolen from more important topics. If the learner is to feel comfortable and valued, he must feel that you attach importance to this time. Ensure your greeting is positive and that your body language reassures the mentee they are in a safe place and can speak honestly with you.

Be selective when choosing your meeting place. A loud place with lots of distractions is not necessarily a good choice. Neither is a place where there is just the two of you and no background noise.

Think about...

- a conversation you had recently with someone you didn't know very well or maybe someone who is senior to you in your workplace:

  – Did they maintain eye contact?

  – Did they listen to your contributions with attentiveness or were they framing a response while listening to you?

  – How positive were their gestures and tone of voice, and did they indicate an active interest in your contribution?

  – Did you leave the conversation feeling valued and reassured that your points had been taken on board?

Questioning

Selecting the correct type of question can be vital in drawing out relevant information and gaining a positive response from a coach within the mentoring relationship. Questions also help the coach unlock alternative approaches and avenues of thought and, at the same time, allow the mentor to clarify the thought processes of the coach and understand their statements and actions.

Questions can be used for many reasons. All questions are either **closed** or **open**.

Closed Questions

These require a specific and factual answer; for example: 'Do you have a tactical plan for this game?' or 'Are you happy with that performance?' They often direct the responder towards a yes or no answer. These questions may be useful to focus on a particular aspect of coaching. However, closed questions should always be followed with a more open question to allow the coach to express opinion. Closed questions are didactic in approach and can result in a very one-sided conversation. Avoid using too many closed questions consecutively.

Open Questions

These provide no direction for the response; for example: 'What do you think are the attacking strengths of your team?' The danger with open questions is that the conversation loses focus or strays off at a tangent. These questions should therefore be followed by further questions that probe the answer and encourage the coach to focus on the key aspects.

There are a number of methods to **probe** an answer given to an open question.

Funnelling is a technique in which you will increasingly narrow the focus of each question until you arrive at the crux of the issue. It allows you to examine a coach's thought processes and reasoning. You will need to develop skills in phrasing questions that require the coach to give increasingly focused answers, without leading them. Another probing technique, called **drilling**, means asking focused questions that dig progressively deeper into an issue until the required insight/answer is forthcoming. This doesn't mean you have to continue to ask **why** until you have received a satisfactory answer. However, you will need to be inventive with your phrasing of questions if you wish the conversation to be effective and beneficial to the development of the coach.

Questioning is an important skill to master. It helps to engage the coach in reflective self-analysis in a non-directive manner.

Think about...

- situations in which you might practise observation, feedback, listening and questioning skills.

Communication skills are the most important mentoring skills. They can be developed in many different situations.

Summary

To be an effective mentor you will require certain skills. You will possess some of these skills already, they just need fine-tuning. Others, you must work harder to acquire. All these skills are important. You will only observe something if you are looking for it, and you will only be an effective mentor if you can empower coaches to take control of their own learning.

> *Reaching the goal itself may not be as valuable as the experience that can come in making a supreme effort to overcome the obstacles involved.*
>
> Gallwey, 1986

The Importance of Goals

As a coach, you know that improving performance requires action planning. Just as when you plan programmes with your athletes, a coach's action plan springs from an evaluation of his strengths and weaknesses and an analysis of current practice. In other words, the processes of self-reflection and self-profiling lead the action planning.

Coach Profiling

A coach profile is a snapshot of a coach's current self-perception. Coaches often use profiling to help them understand a performer's perceptions of his strengths and weaknesses. A mentor can use the same technique to generate a similar empathy with a coach. A properly completed profile can provide a base from which coach development plans can be built. Figure 5 illustrates a profile completed by a rugby coach.

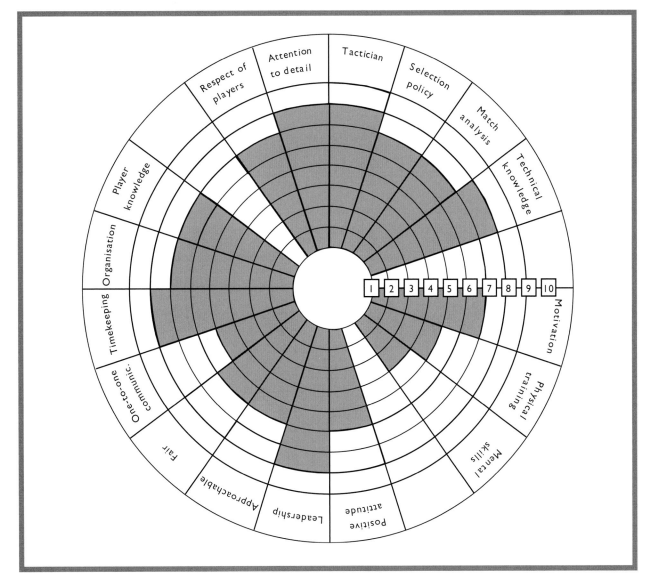

Figure 5: Completed profile of a rugby coach

The profile in Figure 5 illustrates that the coach believes he is strong in the areas of technical knowledge, timekeeping and leadership, but weak in the areas of mental skills, knowledge of physical training and one-to-one communication.

How to Profile

The profiling exercise will be familiar to many sports coaches. The process involves:

1 identifying key components of coaching performance

These must be the important performance components according to the coach – not those you think are important.

2 clarifying the meaning of each component listed by the coach

This has two functions – it can identify the important elements of each component and make it easier for the coach to assess their performance in the component (Step 3), and it can also prevent misunderstandings if terminology is used in slightly different ways by the coach and mentor.

3 self-rating of current performance in each area against a perfect performance

This is usually on a scale of 1–10. This part can be quite difficult. It is usually best not to spend too long at this stage but to tell the coach to think briefly about each one and score as he currently feels appropriate.

4 plotting the coach's profile on a chart.

This provides a concrete depiction of an abstract concept – the coach's self-perception. It can be a useful starting point for development planning. Most importantly, it can help to generate the understanding that is central to a mentoring relationship.

> Photocopy the next three pages and use them to help you generate a profile with each of the coaches you are mentoring. An extra blank copy of each is available in Appendix A.

1 Identifying key components of coaching performance

Think of the qualities required by a good coach and list them below.

When completing this exercise you may find it useful to use the headings **knowledge**, **coaching skills** and **personal qualities**. Some sample qualities are included – delete them if you do not agree.

Category	Components
Knowledge	eg Knowledge of physiology
Coaching skills	eg Planning
Personal qualities	eg Communication, leadership

2 Clarify the meaning of each component listed by the coach

You may wish to expand on your description of some components to avoid confusion.

Use open questions such as: 'What does this mean to you?' or 'How important do you consider this to be?' to gauge the coach's understanding of the components listed.

3 Self-rating of current performance in each area against a perfect performance

List the 20 most important components and rate your current performance in each of these areas from 1–10, where 10 represents total competence.

Component	Rating
	1 2 3 4 5 6 7 8 9 10
	1 2 3 4 5 6 7 8 9 10
	1 2 3 4 5 6 7 8 9 10
	1 2 3 4 5 6 7 8 9 10
	1 2 3 4 5 6 7 8 9 10
	1 2 3 4 5 6 7 8 9 10
	1 2 3 4 5 6 7 8 9 10
	1 2 3 4 5 6 7 8 9 10
	1 2 3 4 5 6 7 8 9 10
	1 2 3 4 5 6 7 8 9 10
	1 2 3 4 5 6 7 8 9 10
	1 2 3 4 5 6 7 8 9 10
	1 2 3 4 5 6 7 8 9 10
	1 2 3 4 5 6 7 8 9 10
	1 2 3 4 5 6 7 8 9 10
	1 2 3 4 5 6 7 8 9 10
	1 2 3 4 5 6 7 8 9 10
	1 2 3 4 5 6 7 8 9 10
	1 2 3 4 5 6 7 8 9 10
	1 2 3 4 5 6 7 8 9 10

4 Plotting the coach's profile on a chart

Now insert the components in the outer section of the chart. Indicate the score in that component by shading the required number of sections. Use Figure 5 as a guide if you are unsure.

Performance profile of: _____   Date: _____

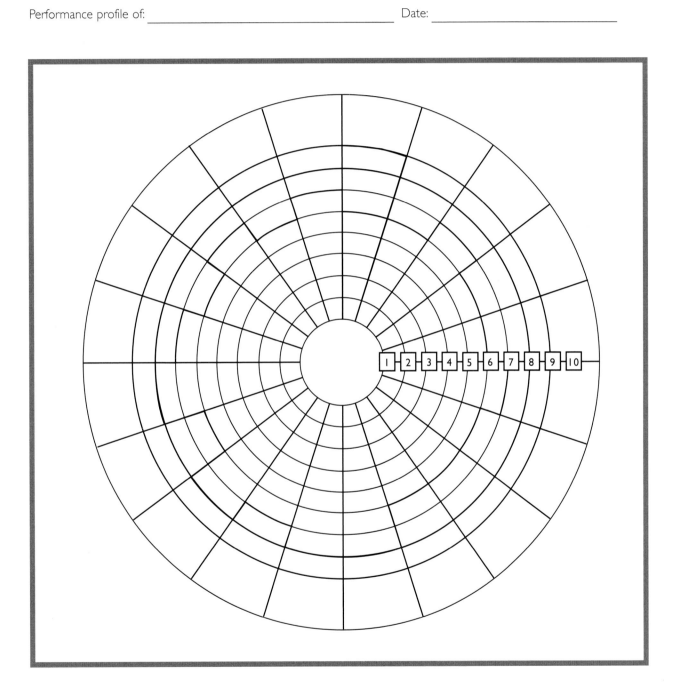

The completed profile is a representation of the coach's self-perception. It indicates the coach's strengths and weaknesses as they appear to them. You may have different opinions of the strengths and weaknesses, and you may disagree on the ratings the coach has given himself in some areas. That is immaterial. The profile is not intended to provide an objective assessment of performance. It is a tool that may be used to generate a shared understanding of self-concepts and priorities.

When Should I Suggest a Profile?

Because coach profiling is at the centre of development planning and of generating empathy between mentor and coach, the earlier a profile is attempted the better. The profile is likely to change considerably in the early stages as the coach comes to terms with the profiling concept and grows to trust the mentor. The profiling process can be repeated numerous times within a mentor:coach relationship as the coach's practice evolves.

Flexibility

The completed profile is an organic chart – it changes in shape and content as the coach develops. The changing profile of the coach should be recorded in the coach's portfolio, with the logbook and reflective journal. The intervals between profiling exercises should be discussed by the mentor and coach. Profiling should be attempted when the coach believes there will be significant differences between the previous chart and the current one.

Development Planning

In the next section, you will look at development planning for coaches. The profile will be used as the basis for this plan. It can be used for this purpose even though it is not an objective measure of performance. Indeed, many coach educators would question the possibility of providing a completely objective assessment tool for coaches. The profile is used for development planning because the goals set and timescales outlined are based on a framework with which the coach can identify. The areas prioritised will be those the coach has identified for herself. The whole process will be relevant to the coach, who is therefore more likely to adhere to it.

Coach Profiling and Assessment

The profiling tool should not be used as an assessment tool. It is not intended to be an objective measure of any set of coaching competences. If your role as mentor includes an assessment role (see Section Eight for a brief discussion of the difficulties of this dual role), you will need to use a set of competences preordained by the awarding organisation for this assessment. National standards attempt to standardise coaching competences across levels and across sport and are likely to be the basis of any such set of competences.

In such a situation, you might like to use the profiling exercise to lead into the discussion of the required standards. Compare the components of coaching performance identified by the coach in the profiling exercise with those outlined in the assessment criteria. The comparison might demonstrate to the coach how her performance or priorities needed to change in order to succeed in the assessment. In any case, the discussion will allow you to explain the criteria that you must use in the assessment.

Identifying Priorities

Having identified the strengths and weaknesses of the coach through a profiling exercise, the next task is to prioritise the areas for improvement. The scores on the profiling chart, coupled with the perceived importance of each component, will lead to some very clear indications about areas that need to be improved. The coach must now set development goals in these areas.

The profiling chart can be used to set priorities among the many components of coaching performance. Ask the coach to mark on the performance profile the ratings they would like to have achieved in each component in 12 months' time. This will identify a performance gap in some components of performance. A development plan can then be outlined to close that gap.

The performance profile is both a snapshot of the coach's current self-perception and an illustration of her aspirations. Over time, it becomes a record of progress. The profile should now look like the one in Figure 6 where our rugby coach (see page 25) has indicated that, as a priority, he would like to improve his competency (knowledge, understanding and application) of three areas over the coming 12 months (physical training, mental skills and one-to-one communication – see darker shaded areas).

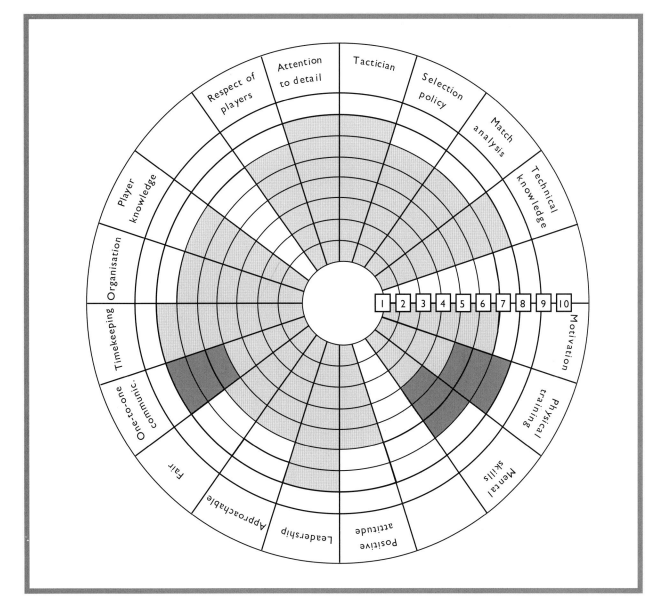

Figure 6: The performance profile showing the most important performance

Goal Setting

Goal setting focuses on closing the gaps in performance identified by the profiling exercise. It is now an accepted part of development planning and most people are familiar with the process. The following panel will serve as a reminder of the principles of goal setting:

In general, all goals should be:

Specific

They must be directly relevant to the needs of the coach.

Measurable

Quantifiable goals can be measured and assessed.

Acceptable

Coaches must believe they can achieve their goals.

Realistic

Goals should be challenging, but within the coach's capability.

Time-phased

Each goal should have a specific timescale in which to be achieved.

Exciting

Coaches should be pleased and excited about achieving their goals.

Recorded

Goals should be recorded for mentor and coach reference.

Setting SMARTER goals is easier in some areas than in others. It is easy to set goals relating to routine tasks (eg to be five minutes early for all sessions/meetings). It is much more difficult to set goals that focus on a component of a personal quality such as leadership skills. By focusing on what the coach must do (actions), it is usually possible to phrase them according to SMARTER principles. The subjective score from the performance profile can be used to set goals and track progress in these situations.

The Development Plan

The goal-setting process should form the basis of a development plan, which should be completed by the coach **in consultation with** the mentor. The long-term goals set using the performance profiling tool will be the basis for short- and medium-term goals. A development plan outlines these goals and the process by which they are to be attained, including courses, home study, reading, experiential learning, tasks to be undertaken, observations of others and so on.

Examine the development plan based on the goal of improving feedback skills. The coach is concerned that his on-field communication with his athletes is rather ineffective – he does a lot of shouting with very little obvious return. He has identified the following steps towards achieving his goal of 70% effectiveness in communication:

Table 4: Goal setting

Long-term Goal	Short-/Medium-term Goals	Process
By January, to have improved communication with my performers so I can rate myself at 70% effective in this area.	To increase the number of individual feedback statements by 20% and to decrease the number of group/general feedback statements by the same amount by September.	To record the number of ineffective feedback remarks made at each coaching session for the next two weeks and to categorise the ineffectiveness into content or context problems.
	To decrease the total amount of feedback statements in each coaching session by half by the end of December.	To video a coaching session and to analyse the content and context of the interaction between myself and the players.
		To attend the sports coach UK workshop 'Analysing Your Coaching' by February.

Use the planner on the next page to complete a development plan with a coach. Remember that the development goals should focus on the areas planned for in the performance profile.

A blank development planner is available in Appendix A so that you can photocopy it for future use.

Tip

Do not attempt to develop too many areas simultaneously. The coach will still need to focus primarily on the task of developing performers. One self-development area is usually all that is possible to target at any one time.

Development Plan

Long-term Goal	Short-/Medium-term Goals	Process Goals	Achieved	Comment

© Alan Edwards

The Coach's Portfolio

The coach's profile, development planner and coaching log are tools that demonstrate the development of the coach and the mentoring relationship. It may be useful for the coach to keep a development portfolio or development log containing all these documents. The portfolio should also include evidence of attendance at coach education courses. If the mentoring process needs to be evaluated at some stage, this portfolio is a useful illustration of the benefits of mentoring. If the coach is working towards a governing body of sport award or another qualification, this information should be maintained in the relevant portfolios being produced for these purposes.

Summary

The performance profile is a useful tool for setting the agenda in mentor:coach relationships. The important factor is that this agenda is created by and for the coach. Your role is one of facilitator and helper. One of the key

tasks for the mentor is to ensure any development programme is relevant to the coach's stated goals and priorities.

The profile can be used to identify performance gaps. Goal setting and action planning can then be put in place to close these gaps. A development plan can provide both the coach and mentor with achievable targets. As with athletes, coaches who can see their coaching improving in small and measurable steps will be motivated to work harder towards their self-development goals.

Think about...

- how often a coach should return to her development plan

- who should keep the development plan – the coach or the mentor?

Notes

> *Fortunately, most children learn to walk before they can be told how to by their parents. As a result, children not only learn how to walk very well, but they gain confidence in the natural learning process which operates within them.*
>
> Gallwey, 1986

Everyone is Different

Fortunately for those involved in all types of education, not everybody learns in the same way. If there was a uniform learning style, all those who currently support learning could be replaced by television screens or robots. This does not make the mentor's task any easier. If you are to help coaches to learn most effectively, it is really useful to know and understand learning theory.

Have you noticed that some people like to learn by doing, others by watching? When presented with a new skill some learners will immediately want to try it out. They will probably not make a very good first attempt but will improve gradually as they have more attempts. At the other end of the scale, some learners will want to watch numerous demonstrations before attempting the skill for themselves. They will want to get a feel for the whole of the skill and how all the pieces fit together before attempting to perform it.

Perhaps you have also noticed that some people like to think in abstract theories, while others prefer to rely on their instinct to solve problems. Some will attempt to work out the solutions to problems in a rational way, while others are more likely to go with what feels right or what has worked for them in the past. These differences occur because there are different learning preferences. There are many ways of explaining these differences, and much research has been conducted in an attempt to define individual learning styles. One method of categorisation was devised by Kolb (1984) and is explained here.

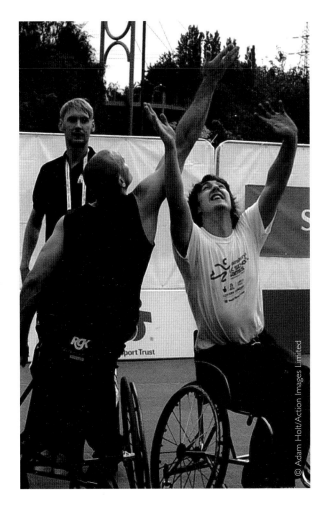

© Adam Holt/Action Images Limited

While many theorists describe a similar process to learning, this model pioneered by David Kolb, known as the experiential learning theory, comprises two components – a four-stage learning cycle and four styles or preferences for learning.

The Learning Cycle

Expressed as a four-stage process, it presents learning as a cyclical process people go through as they attempt to understand and make sense of their experiences. In simple language, the learning cycle can be expressed using the terms feeling, watching, thinking and doing (described below). Coaches can enter at any stage, but all stages must be followed in sequence for successful learning to occur.

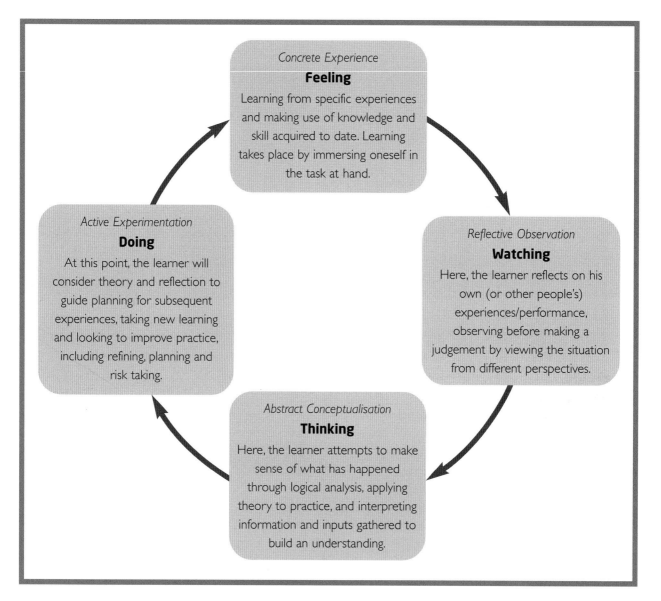

Concrete Experience
Feeling
Learning from specific experiences and making use of knowledge and skill acquired to date. Learning takes place by immersing oneself in the task at hand.

Active Experimentation
Doing
At this point, the learner will consider theory and reflection to guide planning for subsequent experiences, taking new learning and looking to improve practice, including refining, planning and risk taking.

Reflective Observation
Watching
Here, the learner reflects on his own (or other people's) experiences/performance, observing before making a judgement by viewing the situation from different perspectives.

Abstract Conceptualisation
Thinking
Here, the learner attempts to make sense of what has happened through logical analysis, applying theory to practice, and interpreting information and inputs gathered to build an understanding.

Figure 7: The learning cycle

The theory suggests it is insufficient to have an experience in order to learn. It is necessary to review and reflect on the experience to conclude and make generalisations and formulate plans that can then be applied to new situations.

Learning Styles

It is frequently noted that people favour particular methods of interacting with, taking in and processing information during the learning process. Some people like lectures, some like to do something, and others like to go away and read about things or listen to someone, although we often prefer a combination of these. Kolb's learning theory describes four different learning styles:

- converger

- diverger

- assimilator

- accommodator.

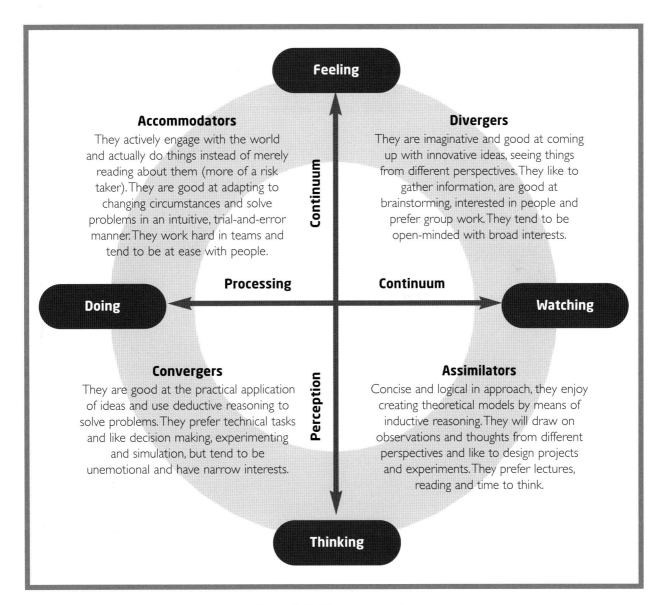

Figure 8: Kolb's learning styles

You may notice similarities between the work of Kolb and that of Honey and Mumford (1986, cited in McGill and Beaty, 1995). There is close alignment between the presentation of the learning cycle and characteristics associated with the learning styles (see Table 5 overleaf). Both theories present learning as a cyclical process and describe the behaviours and characteristics of learners in terms of preferences for engaging with learning.

Table 5: The learning cycle and learning styles

Kolb	Honey and Mumford
Learning Cycle	
• Concrete experience • Reflective observation • Abstract conceptualisation • Active experimentation	• Having an experience • Reviewing the experience • Concluding from the experience • Planning the next steps
Learning Styles	
• Accommodator • Diverger • Assimilator • Converger	• Activist • Reflector • Theorist • Pragmatist

The most important point to remember is that these categories are not intended to be distinct and discrete boxes into which people can be grouped. They are merely a framework that can help you to understand the different ways in which learners approach new material and situations. Most people are quite capable of learning using different learning styles but will also have a preferred learning style and will feel most comfortable approaching new material according to this.

It is important for a mentor to be aware of a coach's likely reaction to new ideas. Unfamiliar material and ideas will place learners under a certain amount of pressure – they will tend to revert to their preferred learning style under this pressure. It may be useful on occasions to get learners to operate outside the comfort zone of their preferred learning style. As a mentor, you should encourage coaches to challenge themselves in their reactions to new ideas.

Your Learning Style

Do you know your own preferred learning style? The following exercise can help you to understand how you approach new ideas. You might like to use it with some of the coaches you mentor so they can come to a similar understanding (if so, photocopy it before you complete it). Try to decide how each of the statements in the following boxes refer to you. Put a '4' in the box next to the statement that is closest to your style; a '3' to the next closest; a '2' to the third closest; and a '1' to the statement that least resembles your style.

Table 6: The learning styles inventory (adapted from Kolb, 1984)

	A		B		C		D	
1	I like to get involved.		I like to take my time before acting.		I am particular about what I like.		I like things to be useful.	
2	I like to try things out.		I like to analyse and break things into parts.		I am open to new experiences.		I like to look at all sides of the issues.	
3	I like to watch.		I like to follow my feelings.		I like to be doing things.		I like to think about things.	
4	I accept people and situations the way they are.		I like to be aware of what is around me.		I like to evaluate.		I like to take risks.	
5	I have gut feelings and hunches.		I have a lot of questions.		I am logical.		I am hard-working and get things done.	
6	I like concrete things that can see, smell, touch and feel.		I like to be active.		I like to observe.		I like ideas and theories.	
7	I prefer learning in the here and now.		I like to consider things and reflect on them.		I tend to think about the future.		I like to see the results of my work.	
8	I have to try things for myself.		I rely on my own ideas.		I rely on my own observations/ideas I have seen others use.		I rely on my feelings – I seem to know what works.	
9	I am quiet and reserved.		I am energetic and enthusiastic.		I tend to reason things out.		I am responsible about things.	

Use the grid below to summarise your score on the learning styles inventory. Write down the score you have given yourself beside the appropriate number, then total each column:

Concrete Experience (like getting involved)		Reflective Observation (like listening and watching)		Abstract Conceptualisation (like thinking and creating ideas)		Active Experimentation (like planning and making decisions)	
1A		1B		2B		2A	
2C		2D		3D		3C	
3B		3A		4C		6B	
4A		6C		6D		7D	
8D		8C		8B		8A	
9B		9A		9C		9D	
Total		Total		Total		Total	

Note: Only put down the marks you have been asked for. You will notice the marks for 1C and 1D are not asked for. This is intended to stop 'patterning' and is not a mistake.

Think about...

You will probably have a higher score in one or two styles. Reflect for a moment on whether your preferred learning style has a significant impact on the way you learn. Might there be occasions when you would be better adopting another style but do not feel comfortable with it? Many coaches depend on one style of learning and so find it difficult to get maximum benefit from potential learning situations.

It is important to note that there is no best learning style. Those who can learn in a variety of ways are able to choose the style best suited to the material in question. Helping a learner develop new learning styles may be an important part of learning, so learning styles could well be a fruitful topic for mentors to explore with coaches.

Style Conflict

An understanding of how learning styles differ can help you towards a better understanding of the coach you are mentoring. There is potential for conflict if your preferred learning style is in stark contrast to that of the coach. Could you understand a reflector's reluctance to try out new ideas immediately if your style tends to be activist, for example? Alternatively, a reflective mentor might become quite annoyed at a coach who seems to jump in and try new ideas before she has a complete understanding of them. Mentors and coaches can easily become frustrated by the different styles in which each approaches new material.

Think about...

- selecting a learning style quite different to your own

- a potential problem when dealing with someone who tends towards this style; explain how you would deal with this:

Summary

Learning is not just about accumulating information or discovering new ideas. It is about reshaping current practice to take these new ideas into account. People choose to deal with new information in different ways according to their preferred learning style. It is important for mentors to understand how individuals differ and to be able to empathise with learners in their approaches to new material.

Please note that some caution is needed when examining the theory of learning style. There has been concern expressed recently (Coffield et al. 2004a; 2004b) that practitioners and researchers have become fixed in their approach to understanding and applying these. Research is ongoing in this area. For further coach learning-related material, see Cushion et al. (2010) for a useful summary. It should also be highlighted that this is only one aspect of learning theory.

Notes

There is a natural learning process which operates within everyone – if it is allowed to. The process is waiting to be discovered by all those who know of its existence.

Gallwey, 1986

Self-reflection Process

Self-reflection is a process that can help coaches learn from experience, regardless of their stage of development. It provides a framework to structure a coach's thoughts on a new experience in such a way that the learning potential of the experience is maximised. The self-reflection process is the link between theory and practice, as described in Section One. It is central to all learning and should help you manage and structure all your meetings with a coach.

Coaches are limited in this process by two constraints:

*   It is a time-consuming process. Because of the nature of their work, coaches do not often have the time to spend on extensive self-reflection. However, as coaches become familiar with the process, it will become less time-consuming.

*   Coaches are limited by the extent of their own experiences. Coaches who lack experience in coaching may not find it easy to move outside their perceptions of what coaching entails and how it should be done.

A mentor is essential to the process of self-reflection.

Mentors can:

*   create an atmosphere where coaches are encouraged to challenge the way they currently do things

*   help to refine the process of self-reflection and keep it on track in the early stages so it is not too time-consuming

*   move the coaches outside the frame of their own experience – they may do this by giving feedback; that is, making suggestions, directing learners to sources of information, or encouraging coaches to experiment with new ideas.

Self-reflection is a learning tool that allows coaches to take responsibility for their own development. It is a key skill for the coach. Once a coach has mastered the process, she can maximise the learning potential in any situation, relating broad principles to specific instances. Self-reflection can help a coach to keep learning through a lifetime of coaching.

The Self-reflection Cycle

All self-reflection requires a catalyst to spark the process. This catalyst is usually an experience related to coaching. As a mentor, you may wish to create this experience (eg by inviting a coach to attend a competition with you), or you may attend a coaching event organised by the coach (eg a training session or planning session).

Self-reflection begins and ends with the coach's own practice. Reflection should always occur post-experience and should relate directly to that experience. The structure of self-reflection is outlined in Figure 9 overleaf.

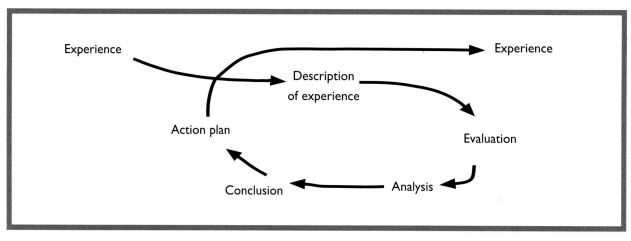

Figure 9: The self-reflection cycle (adapted from Gibbs, 1988)

Reflection should occur as soon as possible after the **experience**, so events are fresh in the memory of both coach and mentor. Use questioning to help the coach move through the different steps of the self-reflection cycle. Carefully phrased questions are key to provoking meaningful reflection. Allow the coach to lead the discussion.

The first step in the reflective process is for the coach to **describe** the experience in a non-evaluative way. This helps the coach to move from their initial subjective reaction to the experience to a more objective perspective. Objectivity is necessary for the self-reflection to be effective.

The coach should then outline what was effective and useful (**evaluation**) in the performance or the experience. At this stage he should avoid being analytical. Evaluating means stating the aspects of the experience or problem that were effective (and ineffective) relative to the predetermined goals – sorting out what worked from what did not.

In the **analysis** of these (searching for reasons), a coach gains an insight into their own strengths and weaknesses, which helps inform a **conclusion** about their own coaching practice. This stage of the process may shed some light on the solution to the problem. It is just as likely that the coach will identify an area in which his knowledge is insufficient to take the investigation further. In this case, the action plan will be either to develop knowledge in this area or to look for help from external sources.

The self-reflection then always returns to the coach's own practice in the form of **action** points for development – to be implemented in the next session, or as soon as possible afterwards. The plan may be to try a new coaching method, or to search for more information on a certain topic. The important point is that the plan must have a direct effect on the behaviour of the coach.

The efficacy of these action points will then form the starting point for further reflection.

> At this stage the reflection may be informed by new information or input from an external source. The main limitation on self-reflection is the experience of the coach. Coaches must move outside the boundaries of their own experience if they are to develop. Your contribution to the process can be invaluable – to challenge the assumptions and beliefs that underpin the coach's reasoning.

The Mentor's Role in Reflection

As a mentor, your primary role is to facilitate this process. Your role will change as the coach moves through the different stages of reflection.

Table 7: The mentor's role in supporting reflection

Stage of Reflective Cycle	Mentor Role
Description	Listening and questioning
Evaluation	Questioning
Analysing	Challenging
Concluding	Directing and assisting
Action planning	Clarifying

Remember, the coach must always take the lead in the reflection process. Your task as mentor is to help coaches with their reflection, encourage them to challenge their current thinking and ensure they have the confidence to use new information to change their coaching practice. By careful questioning, you can lead the coach through the process without influencing the content.

Self-reflection is an important process for coaches to master. It is essential that a coach mentor understands the process thoroughly. For further information on self-reflection, and some practice in applying it to your development as a mentor, see Section Eight.

Self-reflection is about embedding the search for feedback into the coaching process, in a continuous search for improvement. In industry, the Japanese call the search for continuous improvement 'Kaizen'. They attempt to make this process a part of day-to-day operations – not just in a reaction to a crisis. This should be your aim as a mentor.

Self-reflection and Learning Styles

Coaches with different learning styles may require different levels of support at different stages in the reflective cycle. Consider the following examples:

Might divergers (or reflectors) use the reflective cycle automatically? What area might they need help with? Perhaps the movement from action planning to action?

The accommodator (or activist) might be too inclined to skip the analysis stage and may tend to move from evaluation into action without a pause for thought.

Convergers (or pragmatists) may limit the alternatives open to them in the conclusion stage – they may need encouragement to move outside the bounds of their own experience to be creative in their approach to solving problems.

Assimilators (or theorists) may tend to agonise over the analysis stage – they may need help to draw some conclusions from what might appear to them to be limited information.

There are different implications for different learning styles at different stages of the reflective cycle. For each style, move through the stages of the cycle and predict where each might have problems, as well as the areas that would come naturally.

	Should Be Good At...	**Might Need Help With...**
Diverger		
Accommodator		
Assimilator		
Converger		

Reflective Journals

Many coaches use a journal to assist them in the process of reflection. Such a journal helps to structure the reflective process by guiding the coach through the reflective cycle. It is useful to structure a journal so that important cue questions are posed to the coach at each stage (see Table 8).

Table 8: Self-reflection questions

	Core Question: What information do I need access to in order to learn from this experience?
1	Describe the important detail of the session. What are the key points for reflection in this experience?
2	Reflect on what you were trying to achieve. How effective were your actions in achieving this end?
3	Examine your motivation for your actions. What sources of knowledge/information influenced your actions? Where was your knowledge deficient? How can you address this?
4	Could you have dealt with the task in a different way? What other options did you have? Explore the consequences of one of these.
5	How will you change your future actions in the light of this and past experience?

A journal can help develop the habit of reflection and should be completed by a coach as soon as possible after each coaching session. As time passes, recording emotions or thoughts becomes more difficult.

A reflective journal can easily be combined with a coach's logbook, but the two should not be confused. Many coaches are required to keep a logbook of their coaching hours for qualification programmes. These are usually submitted at the end of a year or a required number of coaching sessions. A reflective journal is a private record of reflection. It should always remain the private property of the coach. Coaches should be allowed to disclose only what they think is reasonable in conversation with the mentor.

In combining the two, the perceived workload is reduced. A formula that appears to work is to include a logbook page and a journal page on two adjacent pages of the same notebook. The sections to be submitted for assessment can then be photocopied when required.

It may be useful to divide the adjacent pages into two sections, one for description and one for reflection. It is important, however, that you allow the coach to find the method and style of reflection that best suits her.

Reflection is not an easy process. The difficulties are aptly summarised in the following reflection by a student nurse[2]:

[2] Self-reflection is established as a key area in the education and training of nurses and other medical professions.

I've been thinking recently about how difficult it is to be reflective...I often feel like I don't have enough time to step back and evaluate how effective I am. By the time I finish one day, I usually feel like there is still next day's mountain to climb. Another thing about reflection – it's hard. It's hard because one must analyse what's transpired and to some degree make a value judgement about it. And if the reflection is honest, it can mean that I may have to alter my style or completely chuck something that I have worked hard to develop. It seems to be much safer and secure not to reflect, because I don't have to change that which I don't see as wrong.

Saylor, 1990

Reviewing the Journal

The process of reflection occurs after every session, but similar themes will be addressed in many of the reflections. The journal therefore becomes a subjective record of the development of a coach. Coaches should be encouraged to review their journals frequently and to update their reflections by adding notes in at a later stage. Every entry should be dated. In this way, the coach will be able to track the progress of her thoughts and reflection on a particular issue.

The best format for any reflective journal is a matter of personal preference. As coaches become familiar with the process, many use a Dictaphone to record their immediate thoughts. Others prefer to take time over a journal that is structured in a similar way to the sample questions outlined earlier. Coaches should experiment until they find the process most beneficial to them.

How Can the Mentor Help?

The task of the mentor is to facilitate the self-reflection process – to make it easier for learners to learn from their own experiences. That is not to say a mentor will tell the coach what he is doing wrong. Mentors must not assume they know what coaches need as this will result in cloning, rather than a learning process. Mentors must allow coaches to develop in the way that best suits them as individuals. Each learner will have his own learning style and preferred coaching style, which may be very different from that of the mentor.

The self-reflection process should shape the relationship between the mentor and the learner. The key stages in the process are shown in the following table:

Table 9: Self-reflection key stages

Key Stage	Mentor Role
1 Coaching activity – description of experience/problem	Objective observer/listener
2 Evaluation	Objective listener; probing
3 Analysis	Challenging
4 Conclusion	Clarifying source of knowledge and/or objective feedback
5 Development planning	Adviser; confidence builder

The first step for the mentor is to share coaching experience with the coach. This experience could be anything from planning a session together to the more formal observation of the coach taking a session.

You should then help the coach with the reflective practice model, using either the self-reflection cycle (Figure 9) or the self-reflection questions (Table 8) as a framework. It may be useful to use either of these to explain your aims to the coach. This reflection is most likely to take the form of a conversation between you and the coach, but you may wish to simply prepare the coach for the process and allow her to proceed. In the latter case, you would need to be available for assistance at every stage in the process – this is where phone calls and emails become useful communication vehicles. The model may be used to guide a written reflection by the learner (a reflective journal). The learner may be more comfortable in the journal mode while she comes to terms with the process.

Your role is very important throughout the process. The coach leads the reflection, but your task is to guide the coach, to listen and to ensure that both you and the coach are clear on the meaning of the coach's reflections. You are ideally placed to offer feedback on the effectiveness of the development plan by observing the learner periodically and assisting with plans for further development.

Summary

Self-reflection is a process by which learners analyse their own practice, evaluate it and plan to improve it. All learners do it, but because of their inexperience and unfamiliarity with the process, they may not do it as effectively as they could. The role of the mentor is to assist in the process. A successful mentor will lead the process but will continually seek to empower the coach. Your ultimate aim as a mentor is to render yourself obsolete.

Think about...

- how the model for self-reflection applies in the following situations:

    – mentor and coach observing a competition together

    – mentor and coach planning a programme.

Notes

I was once asked 'In a conversation between a fool and a wise man, who learns the most?' The fool is a fool because he doesn't know how to learn from experience; the wise man is wise because he does. Therefore the wise man will learn more from the conversation than the fool.

Gallwey, 1986

Qualities of a Mentor

There is no ideal profile of a mentor any more than there is a pattern for the perfect mentoring relationship. In Section Three the skills necessary for mentoring were outlined. Some personal qualities can help you put these skills to best use. Reflect on the extent to which you possess the qualities outlined in the following panel.

Empathy – Can you see things from the coach's viewpoint? Are you able to facilitate and empower coaches without forcing your style or point of view on them?

Patience – Can you avoid giving excessive direction and allow the coach to learn at his own pace?

Objectivity – Are you able to see the benefit of other approaches to problems and realise that your way is not the only one?

Time – Do you have the time to give a coach a proper mentoring experience?

Knowledge – Do you have (or have access to) sources of knowledge that the coach does not?

Experience – Have you undergone the process the coach is going through? Can you see the bigger picture?

Challenger – As a mentor you must be ready to challenge preconceived beliefs and practices, both of yourself and the coach.

These and other qualities are required to various degrees by mentors. You may believe you have some and not others – this does not mean you cannot mentor, nor does it mean you will not be a good and effective mentor. As coaches have different coaching styles, so mentors achieve similar ends by different means.

Self-profiling

As a mentor, you will be pursuing the same path of continuous development that you promote to coaches. In order to maximise every learning opportunity that will make you a better mentor, you will need to reflect on your mentoring experiences and analyse your current practice. Just as a coach can find a clearer perspective on her development by profiling strengths and weaknesses, you should profile yourself in the mentoring role.

The next few pages guide you through this process.

List the important knowledge (eg learning styles), skills (eg questioning) and personal qualities (eg empathy) required by a mentor, in your opinion:

Knowledge		Skills		Qualities	

Clarify the meaning of each one to your own satisfaction:

. . . .

. . . .

. . . .

. . . .

. . . .

. . . .

. . . .

. . . .

. . . .

. . . .

Now rate yourself in each component of mentoring performance on a scale of 1–10, where 10 represents absolute competence in the component.

Fill in the following blank profile wheel:

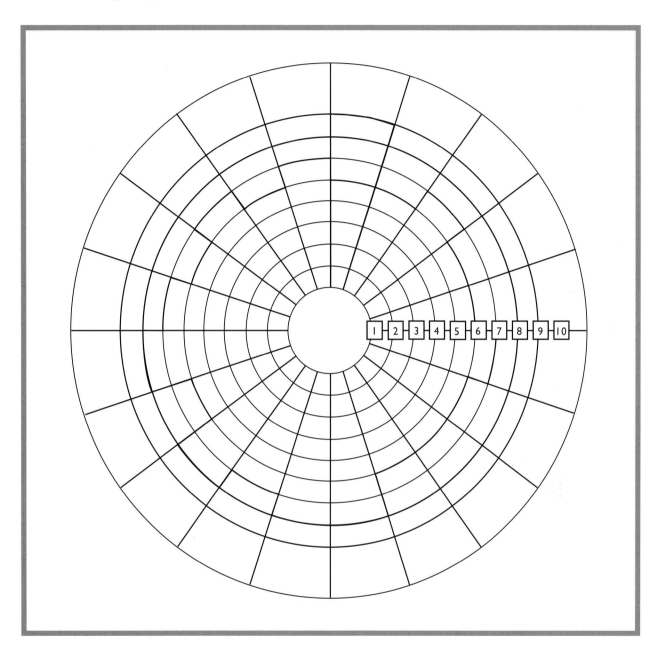

For each component, indicate the score you would like to achieve in 12 months' time.

Mark this on the profile using a dotted line.

Select one area you will prioritise for development. Set yourself a 12-month goal for this component.

Then set short- and medium-term goals that will assist you to achieve that goal.

Identify the processes by which you will endeavour to develop your skills/qualities and set process goals in these areas.

Long-term Goal	Short-/Medium-term Goals	Process

Evaluating Mentoring

It is important you gain feedback from the coach on your role as mentor. The extent to which your contribution has been valued by the coach will be the acid test of the relationship. It will inform you as to how successful you have been in your attempts to make your relationship relevant to the coach's agenda, and how effective the relationship has been in working towards the expressed development goals of the coach.

It will be too late if you discover at the evaluation stage that the agenda you have been working to has been perceived by coach and mentor in different ways. In Section Two, the importance of clarifying expectations, agreeing priorities and setting goals was emphasised. If

this step has not been sufficiently well established, you may well find the expectations of the coach have not been met by your actions as the mentor.

Much of the feedback you will require should be available in the general conversations you will have in the normal course of the relationship. However, it is useful to have a formal evaluation process at some stage in the relationship to enable a detailed and comprehensive review of its effectiveness. If your relationship is part of a formal mentoring programme, such an evaluation may be a requirement of the programme. In Appendix C there are some mentoring tools to help you. These can be used to provide a record of the relationship and evaluate its effectiveness from the perspective of the coach and the mentor.

Summary

If you are a good coach, it is likely that you will be a good mentor. The reflective qualities that help you to learn from experience and from others as a coach will stand you in good stead for your role as a mentor. Mentoring is one of the most rewarding roles a coach can fill. The aim of this resource is to help you give and gain the most from your mentoring relationships.

© Alan Edwards

Notes

You may photocopy the tools provided here to assist your mentoring programme. Adapt them to any format that suits both you and the coach you are mentoring.

Profiling Tools

1 Identify key components of coaching performance.

Think of the qualities required by a good coach and list them below:

Category	Components
Knowledge	
Coaching skills	
Personal qualities	

2 Clarify the meaning of each component through mentor/coach discussion. You may wish to expand on your description of some components to avoid confusion:

3 List the 20 most important components and rate your current performance in each of these areas from 1–10, where 10 represents total competence:

Components	Rating
	1 2 3 4 5 6 7 8 9 10
	1 2 3 4 5 6 7 8 9 10
	1 2 3 4 5 6 7 8 9 10
	1 2 3 4 5 6 7 8 9 10
	1 2 3 4 5 6 7 8 9 10
	1 2 3 4 5 6 7 8 9 10
	1 2 3 4 5 6 7 8 9 10
	1 2 3 4 5 6 7 8 9 10
	1 2 3 4 5 6 7 8 9 10
	1 2 3 4 5 6 7 8 9 10
	1 2 3 4 5 6 7 8 9 10
	1 2 3 4 5 6 7 8 9 10
	1 2 3 4 5 6 7 8 9 10
	1 2 3 4 5 6 7 8 9 10
	1 2 3 4 5 6 7 8 9 10
	1 2 3 4 5 6 7 8 9 10
	1 2 3 4 5 6 7 8 9 10
	1 2 3 4 5 6 7 8 9 10
	1 2 3 4 5 6 7 8 9 10
	1 2 3 4 5 6 7 8 9 10

4 Now insert the components in the outer section of the profile wheel. Indicate the score in that component by shading the required number of sections:

Performance profile of: _____ Date: _____

Self: _____

Signed: _____ Date: _____

Mentor: _____

Signed: _____ Date: _____

Long-term Goal	Short-/Medium-term Goals	Process Goals	Achieved	Comment

Use this form to evaluate the mentoring relationship:

For the Coach

1 Briefly summarise the outcomes of the mentoring relationship (eg goals met, successes, achievements, failures):

....

....

....

....

....

....

2 What aspects (eg activities, interpersonal communications) of the relationship were productive? Were any areas disappointing?

....

....

....

....

....

....

....

3 Please give a brief assessment of your mentor's performance:

....

....

....

....

....

....

....

Use this form to evaluate the mentoring relationship:

For the Mentor

1 Briefly summarise the outcomes of the mentoring relationship (eg goals met, successes, achievements, failures):

. . . .

. . . .

. . . .

. . . .

. . . .

. . . .

2 What aspects (eg activities, interpersonal communications) of the relationship were productive? Were any areas disappointing?

. . . .

. . . .

. . . .

. . . .

. . . .

. . . .

3 General comments:

. . . .

. . . .

. . . .

. . . .

. . . .

. . . .

Clutterbuck, D. (2004) *Everyone Needs a Mentor: Fostering Talent in Your Organisation.* 4th edition. London: Chartered Institute of Personnel Management. ISBN: 978-1-843980-54-4.

Coffield, F., Moseley, D., Hall, E. and Ecclestone, K. (2004a) *Should We Be Using Learning Styles? What Research Has to Say to Practice.* London: Learning and Skills Research Centre. ISBN: 978-1-853389-14-5.

Coffield, F., Moseley, D., Hall, E. and Ecclestone, K. (2004b) *Learning Styles and Pedagogy in Post-16 Learning.* London: Learning and Skills Research Centre. ISBN: 978-1-853389-18-8.

Cushion, C., Nelson, L., Armour, K., Lyle, J., Jones, R., Sandford, R. and O'Callaghan, C. (2010) 'Coach learning and development: a review of literature', www.sportscoachuk.org/review

Douge, B., Alexander, K., Davis, P. and Kidman, L. (1994) *Evaluation of the National Coach Accreditation Scheme.* Australian Coaching Council.

Gallwey, W.T. (1986) *The Inner Game of Tennis.* London: Pan's Books. ISBN: 978-0-330295-13-0.

Gibbs, G. (1988) *Learning by Doing: A Guide to Teaching and Learning Methods.* London: Further Education Unit. ISBN: 978-1-853380-71-6.

Hildebrand, S.D. (2007) 'Building solid work relationships: developing rapport with co-workers', http://deborah-s-hildebrand.suite101.com/building-solid-work-relationships-a33852

Kolb, D.A. (1984) *Experiential Learning: Experience as the Source of Learning Development.* Eaglewood Cliffs, NJ: Prentice Hall. ISBN: 978-0-132952-61-0.

Mehrabian, A. (1968) 'Communication without words', *Psychology Today,* 2 (9): 52–55.

McGill, I. and Beaty, L. (1995) *Action Learning: A Guide for Professional, Management and Educational Development.* 2nd edition. London: Kogan Page. ISBN: 0–749415–34–7.

Parsloe, E. (1995) *Coaching, Mentoring and Assessing: A Practical Guide to Developing Competence.* London: Kogan Page. ISBN: 978-0-749416-70-6.

Peters, T.J. and Waterman, R.H. (1995) *In Search of Excellence: Lessons from America's Best-run Companies.* London: Harper Collins. ISBN: 978-0-006384-02-1.

Saylor, C.R. (1990) 'Reflection and professional education: art, science and competency', *Nurse Educator,* 15 (2): 8–11.

sports coach UK works closely with governing bodies of sport and other partners to provide a comprehensive service for coaches throughout the UK. This includes an extensive programme of workshops, which have proved valuable to coaches from all types of sport and every level of experience. For further details of sports coach UK workshops in your area, contact the sports coach UK Workshop Booking Centre.

sports coach UK
Chelsea Close
Off Amberley Road
Armley
Leeds LS12 4HP
Tel: 0113-274 4802
Fax: 0113-231 9606
Email: coaching@sportscoachuk.org
Website: www.sportscoachuk.org

sports coach UK Workshop Booking Centre
Tel: 0845-601 3054
Email: scukworkshops@sportscoachuk.org

Notes

Notes

Our Vision

What we would like to see

UK coaching excellence enabling all children, players and athletes to follow their dreams, have fun and fulfil their potential.

Our Mission

Why we exist

To support our UK partners to recruit, develop and retain coaches to achieve their participation and performance goals (in the context of The UK Coaching Framework).

Our Strategic Objectives

What we will do

To achieve our mission, we will:

1   champion and drive policy and investment in coaching

2   support and challenge our partners to improve their coaching systems and grow their contribution to a cohesive UK coaching system

3   provide products and services that add value to our partners' coaching systems and their coaches

4   provide research and share good practice that will benefit coaching

5   develop quality leadership, good governance and a skilled team to ensure an effective UK coaching agency.

233 -244

B-3

12886

Brain Biochemistry and Brain Disorders

OF PSYCHIATRY LIBRARY
YDE TERRACE, LEEDS 2

hor

The Library
Education Centre, Royal Surrey County Hospital
Egerton Road, Guildford, Surrey GU2 7XX
Tel: 01483 464137

Class no: WL 348   Computer no: H0004756